Poems that rhyme from my heart

From the end to the start

By David Mondragon

WESTBOW
P R E S S®
A DIVISION OF THOMAS NELSON
& ZONDERVAN

WestBow Press books may be ordered through booksellers or by contacting:

WestBow Press
A Division of Thomas Nelson & Zondervan
1663 Liberty Drive
Bloomington, IN 47403
www.westbowpress.com
1 (866) 928-1240

ISBN: 978-1-9736-7721-5 (sc)
ISBN: 978-1-9736-7722-2 (hc)
ISBN: 978-1-9736-7720-8 (e)

Library of Congress Control Number: 2019915885

Print information available on the last page.

WestBow Press rev. date: 10/23/2019

Contents

Section 3 - Religious Poems

Section 4 - Characters

Section 5 - Political Poems

Section 1

Poems for Children
or Young at Heart

The Friendly Ant

There once was a friendly ant
who wanted to understand what many can't,
my innermost thoughts and what makes me tick,
and my innermost feelings that can sometime make me sick.
It was late one night, early last year,
when he crawled inside my inner ear.
He must have been deep within because the noise of his travel
began to make me unravel.
I was at the brink of losing all
control, when I thought I heard him say, "If you
want me out, you just have to call."
So I thought and thought of what I should say.
Then it clicked he can't hear, but only play.
So I got something I knew he would love
from a nearby shelf just above,
and cost just a little from me,
a tiny drip of the sweetest honey.
I put it in my outer ear,
hoping it would end my terrible fear,
and make his noise finally disappear.
And to my pleasure, and his I'm sure,
he got stuck in the drip and his noise was no more.

The Hunt Goes On

The quickest rat in town lives near me since I can hear his sound ring true,
and I know I must kill him before his damage is through.
The trap will be set with much care
so it will go off with just a brush of his hair.

Although his annoying sounds can be heard anytime of day,
the gross little rodent only comes out at night to hunt and play.
His nasty evening escapades will soon come to an end
along with his daily raids of the food of man's best friend.

His luck will run out as his winning streak
will end and suffer a deadly scar
by a crushing metal bar
which will come down a bit too hard and fast
just like it did on his ancestors in the not too distant past.

I look forward to the sweet awakening sound of the snap from the trap
and knowing that filthy little rat won't be coming back
to spread his dirtiness around my door anymore.

The Curious Moth

There once was a curious moth who was so daring he even got lost.
He was quite young and bold from what I was
told when he went on his expedition,
going where no moth has ever gone and breaking all family tradition.
He wanted to experience pure darkness on purpose
to see if he would become more relaxed or more nervous.
His journey began when he saw a tired man lying
on his side, believing he was sleeping
as he heard a very lazy sigh and saw him with a tightly shut eye.
He thought for awhile and then decided to give his plan a try,
to fly onto him with the least bit of turbulence
so neither would feel even the slightest disturbance.
Next he thought he would crawl into his ear
and wondered when he drew near, if he would feel ultimate bliss
or something he would have much rather of missed.
As the slowest flutter of his wings stopped he
gently landed and then crawled in
where no moth had ever been, deep within the man's inner ear.
It was exciting at first but soon he began to thirst for light.
He naturally tried to reverse his plight,
but couldn't seem to find his way out,
and panicked as the man began to shout! My friend then explained
to me that he called his neighbor, begging for a favor and said,

"Can you get this crazy insect out of my head?"
Soon his pal was in his house asking where was his spouse
but was quickly interrupted by the man in need
as his words seemed to desperately bleed
from his mouth saying, "How on earth are we going to get him out?"
His friend then said without a doubt
"I need a flashlight bud to see how deep this bug really is." As he found
one he quickly shined it down and all around inside the man's ear.
This almost instantly ended all of his fear, while the curious moth knew
exactly what he had to do as he flew directly out of his darkest night
and right up against the glass of the rescuing light.

Section 2

An Introspective of Thoughts and Experiences

A Fun Time

Soon half my vacation will be over
as Easter is this morning.
It was quite a relaxing and interesting stay
here with my parents during Lent.
I must say it was well spent
and so was I
as fish was beginning to come out of my ears and making me almost cry.

Other than that it was all right
since I feel a bit thinner now and much less uptight.
The old house and neighborhood hasn't changed
much, everything looks about the same,
and still sounds about as quiet and peaceful as a gently falling rain.

As long as my trip home goes smoothly I will
truly be considering visiting more often,
even if my dad can't hear half of my talking
and my mom insists I kiss her orthodox church's
floor where others have just been walking.

A Little Love

I sometimes wonder what a little love might bring
into my life. Surely a brighter night
with more reason to sing than to fight.
I've got to make sure this time around
that I'm not taken for granted, only to later be found
abandoned along with a puzzling frown.

A little respect would also be nice to feel,
which I would reciprocate with great zeal
to show I appreciate her warmth and our deal.

Although I may not have as much time to spend
in that lonely open space between serious relationships and friends,
I still will not alter my taste just to quit this
long tiring chase that may never end.

Creating Club Utopia

I'm going to try and create my club utopia
since I'm tired of being in clubs with phobias,
intricate cliques, prerequisites,
and mostly filled by a prejudiced membership.
If you feel the same way
then I hope one day
you will join my club that doesn't snub.

It's going to be a place
where you can relax and create,
write and debate
whatever you choose in a peaceful setting.
It also won't allow you to be forgetting
its purpose
since its service
won't let you lose the relaxing feeling of its atmosphere
which will be clear
that it's in the spirit of fun,
making new friends, venting, and getting to know everyone.

It's going to be a refuge
where you can be heard about any subject and
maybe one you've been deluged
with by the news or your brother. You also won't have the frustration
of not having a chance to speak because you
couldn't reach the radio station.
And what's more
the membership dues will be low and paid at the door
but only when you decide to show for sure.

I guess getting it to start
will be the hardest part, but once it gains some hands to lend
then it may really begin rolling and it may never have an end.

Hey Brother

Hey brother stop throwing everybody all those curves
'cause you're beginning to get on everyone's nerves
When will you come clean and shoot straight?
We're all here and just can't wait.
Hey brother you can come down from the trip you've been on,
we'll still love you even if you think you're too far gone.
When will you realize confidence is all you lack
and you can be yourself when you finally come back.
Hey brother just calm yourself so your heart won't race or skip a beat.
Just look at your face and have a seat.
When will you come into your own?
Maybe you need an old friend to whisper over the phone.
Hey brother you're still number one in my book
no matter what you've said or what you've took.
When will you wake up and finally listen to our plea?
You can do anything in this world when you let
your chains sink to the bottom of the sea,
then for once in your life you will finally be free.

Bring Me Up Slowly

Bring me up slowly 'cause I've been quite lonely,
and its been awhile since I had a woman who
could make me smile and really hold me.
I want this feeling to last
so let's just talk for hours about the future or the past.
Now can you handle that request ?
Can you pass my test?
If so let's go to a quiet place I know.
If not I guess I will stop right here and I'll be
on my way today, back to my search
for the woman who needs to be taken down from her high perch.
Someone who needs my protection
and attention,
who knows my value is true, though others may not see.
The one who does will always be in my heart
without a chance to depart.
So now that I've made myself clear,
are you ready to walk with me away from here?
If you agree to answer my plea
we may have found our destiny.
Some say I come on too strong,
too up front to have a chance at anyone for very long.
And they might be right but I will take the chance that they are wrong
'cause my girl will be customized to me and not to this world.

Strange Power

A strange power came over me
of simultaneous tiredness and energy.
I felt as if I were running through water and about to fall asleep
yet not straining to walk for a continuous week.
I had to let someone know but could not speak,
so I wrote it down and hoped for some soul's belief,
while wondering thoughts remained in the back of my mind
of how long this mystical limbo could be sustained in real time.
Would it be lengthy and free me of all pain or
very brief and just quickly slip away?
So for a test, I just kept writing and hoped for the best
while I was smiling since I felt I was blessed.
But I still wanted to know
did I have the choice to keep it or just let it go.
As I wrote and wrote to challenge this power
I put an imaginary time limit of just one hour,
and in my mind
I thought this would give me the ending sign.
Then soon my time was up and I felt prepared
but still surprised since I was not scared.
When I stopped writing and then started again,
I knew this strange power would stay 'till my end,
especially when I regained my speech and was happy to say
it will always be within my reach anytime of day.

Pep Talk Time

I may not know you but I bet you've got a lot of good ideas
so don't let any naysayers rattle you with any fears.
I say stick with your heartfelt dreams you have today or had long ago,
even though it seems they have slipped away
and can't come back again to grow.
You may think as I once did that your failed
schemes, lack of wealth, or health
is a sign to give up on those dreams by staying in line with the status quo,
like a relative or friend you may know.
The only problem with this
is the simple fact that those dreams can easily resurface
and nag you with regret and self pity
which you may never forget in your small home town or big city.
It may also lead you to taking desperate risks
to avoid having to just exist.
Fights fueled by feeling left out,
like you don't count must be stopped
before possibly losing everything you've got.
So just pursue all you once knew was true to your heart,
while there is still time to make another start
before you may slowly lose your mind part by part.

The Zone

Have you ever been in the zone and felt all
alone but never wanted to get out?
Do you know what I'm talking about?
It's when even an errant shout or word is heard
but nothing can disturb
or knock you out of your world
of total concentration and elation.
It's also when you're being surrounded by lots of people,
then the feeling gets even deeper,
even if most of them may be around
from your own home town.
Nothing can break your great train of thought,
not a mock, an insult or a horn they may have brought.
No one can throw you a curve that catches you off guard
or from you seeing something easy that too many may seem hard.
Have you ever been in that place?
If not I hope and pray it will happen enough
to change any frown on your face
since the feeling in the zone is something you just can't replace
or have to worry of its controlling pace.

Fear Reducer

I'm determined to find a way to make my life work more for me
and others so I can enjoy my money
and not feel ripped off and grumpy.
I like the idea of reducing my skepticism or fear
with the power of knowledge
to help me through whatever was once unclear in college.
I must admit once I gain enough understanding
in the field I want to pursue
I won't see anything that will stop me from whatever I really want to do.
As I put my priorities in order and reach a small or large goal
then I will know it won't be long before I get on a smooth steady roll.

Fresh Start

Would you be so kind to let me borrow your ears
so I can try to lessen your sorrow and reduce your fears.
I can help if you give me a chance
and together we can find answers so you can take a new stance.

Our approach and strategy will take our adversary by surprise,
and our confidence will show with a sparkle in our eyes.
The more you hear from me and me from you
allows the possibilities of anything to come true.
Will you open up and go half way,
so we can start getting things done here today. We can find ways
to choose the right plays
in this game we call life,
as we shed light into places that were once filled with pain and strife.

Remember solutions lie in a fertile field
waiting to overcome a hurdle that once wouldn't yield.
So please don't be shy and hide away,
just ask yourself why and decide to stay.
After awhile you'll see you made the right choice
by the smile on your face and sound of your voice.

My Dream

Sorry for my temper and sometimes bad habits,
but watch how I will cure my ills without any pills or tablets.

The weakness of the world is the catalyst
that will persist
to turn my meekness into a power
that will devour
any reason to abandon a dream
that would otherwise turn sour or unclean.

I'm tired of sitting on the sidelines of life. I feel the need
to try and plant a seed that is fair and right
in a world of greed that is being tormented every day and night.

It's just a matter of time
when I come around and pick up the pieces of a shattered mind
so I won't get down with the regret of what I feel I may have left behind.

Second Wind

I'm so glad I can still reach back and deep within
to make use of my second wind.
In the past when I wasn't involved with anything organized
I would just wither and be hypnotized
with the first feelings of sleepiness in my eyes.
I would even believe I had been satisfied after I had awoken
but really it was just Satan's lies stealing more of my time
leaving me feeling broken and falling more behind.

Naturally it's common sense
that we all must rest
and get enough sleep to regain energy in order to survive
but not so much that we begin to feel half alive
because we haven't accomplished enough to feel satisfied.

This is why I continue to try to be more conscious of what I
have or haven't done so I won't get into a false comfort zone,
then later sadly see how I overlooked opportunities
that were really always being shown.

The Dream

I listened to some old songs and sang along
until they got into my blood and made me strong.
I knew it wouldn't be long before I wrote some of my own.

Then suddenly I saw a woman who looked real sweet
she got in her car and sped down the street, so I got in mine just in time.
I hoped she would stop real soon
so I prayed to the heavens and glanced at the moon,
please Lord let me meet her and maybe someday show her my room.
I'll be good to her you know I will
because I can't take a risk of losing this thrill.

And just about then she stopped at a light,
I took a chance and swerved to the right
as I squeezed to the front of the line,
got a few honks but I didn't mind since I had
more than just a second this time.
I motioned to her to let her window down as I felt like a clown,
so I just followed suit and asked her if she
could pull over and change her root
for some coffee or a salad with some fruit.
I knew it was a shot in the dark,
but I just felt something in my heart.
First she laughed but then said sure
as she sounded so sweet and pure.
The rest is history as they say 'cause were still
together ever since that fateful day.

Scar On Me

When you left, you left some kind of scar on
me, and it's one you just can't see,
but it floats around wild and free in my stubborn memory.
I hate to think of the good times we had
because it ends up leaving me so sorry and sad.
Yes you left some kind of scar on me, well it still remains
without much change.
I sometimes ask,
when will I heal and feel its past?
You left some kind of scar on me
but I can't let this be its final destiny.
I just can't let it stay here to rest and see it get the best of me.
I've got to regain some kind of control
or I'll get sick from watching myself wither and fold.

You left some kind of scar on me, now what will it
take to erase your face from my memory
so I can live on peacefully.
If I ever find the cure to this sick feeling I must endure,
I'll tell you first that's for sure
since I wouldn't want this old scar
on anyone no matter how near to my heart they are or how far.

Ready For Love

I'm ready for love, I'm tired of lust,
I need some affection, I need some trust.
I still do believe in love at first sight,
but unfortunately I don't think the vast majority
might even let it cross their minds,
in these days and times.

I guess I'll just have to take it slow
like most everyone I know
so I don't take a chance to blow
a possible strong romance that may knock on my heart's door
like its done so many times before.

There is one thing I'm sure of,
I'm not going to settle for someone just because I
think she may be close enough for love.
I've learned my lesson well
and know how to hang tough and be alone and almost in hell
if that's what it takes
to avoid anymore tragic life changing mistakes.

Frustration

It all started way down in Costa Rica
where I met a beautiful senorita.
I was on tour but it was a bore
except for her that's for sure.
I wasn't gambling but still lost my shirt and my pants,
forgetfulness came upon me since I was in love but couldn't dance.
I could tell she was the perfect one for me
but I was a grouch because of my injured knee
and mostly just sat on a couch so unwillingly.
I was stuck in a rock and a hard place
and my pain may have been seen by the look on my face
in my lonely day dream that had too much space.
She was my tour guide so I felt I had to hide my feelings inside
or spoil the fun for everyone and even myself if I was denied.
Although I knew this was true,
I felt there was something I just had to do.
So after we all said our goodbyes there was one other way I had to try
where I wouldn't feel awkward or shy.
Everyone on the bus
including my beautiful tour guide exchanged
email addresses without a fuss
or batting of the eye,
for possible future correspondence so anyone could reply.
This made it easy for me to express myself and it
didn't take much time to write a letter
and hoped it would make us both feel better
and no longer alone
if she would read what I was going to send her when I got home.

Graceful Meeting

So often I reminisce even if it's just about one day ago,
whether or not I put on a good or bad show,
or how everything went,
to see if every hour was well spent.
I know it may sound ridiculous to some,
but it's almost a ritual now since to me it's so much fun.

Now just for an example let me give you a brief sample
of what I'm talking about,
to the point where it makes me want to sometimes sing and shout.
Last night is one I will never forget
since I spent it with my choir brothers who
have so much trust and respect.
Those are just two of their great traits
which seemed to jump out and hit me in the face.
And the reason being is simply because I really experienced their grace
as a newcomer to their group,
by making me feel so accepted and comfortable
in fitting right into their loop.

Let Down and Left Out

When you feel let down and left out
and you wish you had someone around who's true and doesn't shout
in need of a fix to be found
for getting off the ground,
then I'd like to meet you. We can plan our escape from this prison cell
which doesn't have any bars or gates but still makes us feel like hell.
I guess when we feel like this we disappoint
others until they say just go away.
So we've got to insist
that we must resist
getting ripped so we don't get lazy with self pity
and start a committee on all our mistakes
and sour grapes.

We've got to continue on our quest to find us in each others arms
without any qualms about speaking our minds
even if we're not politically correct
at least we will be free and direct.
So I hope
we'll both be able to cope
long enough for us to see eye to eye
then there won't be a need for us to search for another girl or guy.

Passionate Feeling

I remember this passionate feeling
and how it sent me reeling.
Back then I used it like a tool
and when I got what I wanted I let it go like a fool.

Now that I'm older I'm going to harness its power
and not let distractions devour
its flame
like it did with yesterdays pain.

I just want to see it all play out
so there will be no doubt
or regret
whether it's my calling or something I would just rather forget.

I'm going to give this passionate feeling every chance I can
so I will finally find out who I really am.

Can't Let Myself Down Anymore

I can't let myself down anymore,
I've just got to pick up the ball and score.
I can't take another lame cop out excuse
to derail me from the truth. This just sets me up for some more abuse.
No I can't let myself down anymore, I've just
got to pick up the ball and score.

I've got to follow my heart with some help from the planning side
of my mind so I won't be denied
this time to clear my conscience of what I
once used to fear and tried to hide.
I've got to give it my all once again.
I must finish what I started way back when I couldn't find a friend,
only free time to chase a dream no matter how
unlikely it would sometime seem
for any chance of it to succeed.

Yes I can't let myself down anymore, it's time
for me to pick up the ball and score.

Change of Pace

What a nice change of pace
to meet someone sweet with style and grace.
Your friendliness and compliments
and unexpected condiments
put a spring right back into the step of the man in blue,
who delighted in your tasteful rescue.
It's people like you that help me get through each and every year
and make me steer
back on track
when the light at the end of the tunnel sometimes
seems so dim and almost black.

Age Not

As some people get a little bit on the old side they usually say
they are not as spry or bold as when they were
running around in their younger days.
I can see all the reasons why this can be,
but personally I'm glad this hasn't yet happened to me.

I would have to say a lot depends on how physically
fit you are and if you are still able
to perform some younger feats that keep you stable
and at peace.
This would obviously increase
your confidence in whatever challenge you might face
and should actually make you feel greater than when
you finished first in some youth group race.
This would simply be true since you could claim,
I can still do it without any pain
and perform it for proof to anyone who may
need a boost in the sun or the rain.

Better Off Or Not ?

Sometimes I wonder would I be better off staying single
or having a significant other. As I go down the
list of pros and cons and benefits
of what I would have and what I would miss,
I see both choices have qualities that are tough to resist.

I still lean a little more towards meeting my soul mate
and hope she won't hesitate
to show her true feelings before it's too late.
I at the same time don't want to become less appealing
by setting up more defenses while getting closer to dealing
with my final expenses.

I also must not get anxious just since I've been living
alone for so long. I can't afford to jump at someone just to
change the sometimes boring course I've been on.

Figuring Me Out

Whenever I'm down
I've found
all I have to do
is follow through
with a good thought.
And no matter how small or simple the action may be
it still can make me happy, but fortunately
not uncontrollably.
The key for me is to keep my poise
when all the outside interference and noise
seems too much
and would otherwise tighten me up.
I see now that I just must replace
any unwanted feeling I face
with something that lightens me up
so I won't react too rough
since I now know when I've had enough
and what rule
I should let come up and follow as if I were in school.
This is so I don't play the fool
and swallow the wrong influence
from even a comforting constituents.
Now that I'm finally learning more about me while still concerning myself
with anyone else
that shows me a little warmness
then I can confess my intermittent awkwardness
with my story.
And they won't have to worry
since mine is about the same or maybe a bit worse. This will help them
traverse down their mountain of pain
and comfortably taking on more blame
in a new light so they can change too
when they see it's really not that difficult to do.

Desert Time

If I lived in the desert and was almost alone
I could play my music until the break of dawn.
No need to worry who I might disturb,
no one else would be around to get on anyones nerves.
I could sing and scream and not feel like a fool
as long as I had a lover then it all would be so cool.

It would also be so peaceful in the desert with you,
I can hardly wait till it comes true.
So now I'm asking you since we've been together for so long,
"Can you come out here and help me sing my song?"
I can play piano while your sweet voice will make me strong.

Oh darling please say that you will
join me in the desert, for a dream we both can fulfill.
I promise it will be unlike any other fantasy,
with us singing, living, and loving in the desert's serenity.

My Calling ?

I want to turn this town upside down,
yeah I want to turn its head all around.
Hey everybody I'm finally coming alive
so maybe now I can lend you a hand if you need help to survive.
I think I've found my calling,
but I won't know for sure until I feel the cure of
someone laughing, or clapping but not stalling to help
me carry on with all my writing and advising.

So please be true with your reaction so I'll
know if I should pursue my goal
to heal others hearts and souls with my God
given art that's begging to unfold.
Thanks to the Lord I have so many stories that I believe need to be told
and may hold the key to set many free from bondages
and insecurities before they get too old.
I hope you will lend me an ear or two so together
we can get on through this life
with a little less pain and a little less strife.

Mystery Man

Will my humorous part of my brain
be able to entertain
on Wednesday? Who will show up the old Dave, the new one,
or will it be someone in between that we've all never seen,
it's still a mystery
even to me.
But whoever does it will be a good time guaranteed for all to enjoy
every man, woman, girl, or boy.
Inspiration is so beautiful when its magic happens. I arise,
look down at my paper and can't believe my eyes
as my pen keeps working overtime.
And of course I don't mind
I just love to watch what will be new
that I can record for all to hear to make them less board or even less blue.
So I hope many will show on time
and maybe even more as the early evening sunshine
slowly passes and goes away, then into tomorrow
and on and on I will continue to write
so more may someday notice my light.

My Key

The key to my life is quality sleep. I know it
may sound too simple and a bit silly
but with it everything heals faster both mentally and physically.
Now when this occurs then obviously my energy would increase
and I'm sure traces of my grouchiness would cease.
Patience and tolerance would reach new heights
and I would begin to lose sight
of how I need to try and prove how right I might be,
since I would then see it's not always so necessary.
I guess the list could go on and on how many
areas of my life would improve
and bad traits I would lose
if I could consistently have quality sleep that would really soothe.
It would surely help me reach all that I desire
without brooding until my temper catches fire.

Always Thinking

I like the stimulation and gratification that goal setting can give
so I'm sure boredom won't seep in with the way I live.
I know I must be careful to protect what I've got and grateful to be able to
feel refreshingly new and never too shot for something important to do.
In my free time I sometimes enjoy doing something that looks fun
and that I've never done,
by going out on a limb
for the sheer pleasure of seeing if I will sink or swim.
Now if I should fail miserably like a misfiring cannon
I don't always abandon
the idea. I just adjust my energies thrust to a different angle
which can often easily untangle
a confusing mess of problems and fear. This repositioning of my approach
is like having a different coach
to help me with solving my challenges. Whether the problem
occurred from something that happened or someone has said
this strategy can really help me solve and satisfy them without any dread.

Renewed Power

I'm so glad that whenever my lack of sleep
decides to creep
up and catch me I'm at home
where I can relax alone
for however long need be.
Even though I know there are people and places I'd like to see,
in the long run everyone would agree if they were in my shoes
they would stop for awhile too, before their
body paid anymore hurtful dues.
In the past I didn't always make this decision
and later found myself in a crash, or sick and
in a very compromising position.
As simple as the solution of more rest and sleep is,
it's still a problem I have trouble to really completely fix.
I'm just grateful I can sense an oncoming
expense when I'm most likely to slip
and know when to avoid certain trips.
At these times I'm happy to have the will to insist
on putting myself on recharge like an electric car
that waits in a garage before it takes a ride whether near or far.

Step Back

Sometimes we all need to take a step back, catch
our breath, and reassess our lives
whether we're single or have husbands or wives
that we may not really
know or hardly ever see.

Whatever is the case our goals
can change when we stare at our face in the mirror
and try to look deeper into our soul
rather than the surface that says we're too young or too old.
Although we can adapt so well to a rather
meager and somewhat hapless life
by telling ourselves that everything is all right
while at the same time we might
know deep down what we need to rearrange.
I guess it's just a matter of how bad do we want change
or how tolerable it is to keep everything the same.

Now if we can get a feel of what kind of new deals with
friends and loved ones could be made for the upgrade
of all involved,
then there will be no end to the problems that can be solved
if we have them in all translations
so more can prosper in future generations.

Work 'n' Play

I don't want anymore overtime.
I just want to go home and ease my mind.
I will then go to that special place
without leaving a trace
of any actual travel,
yet still feel at peace
and miles away from anything that may really baffle and needs to cease.

And all I need for a start
is just a little spark.
It could be from a song I might have heard long ago
but still gets me rolling whether it's fast or slow.
You know what I'm talking about if you can turn
those things you need to get done
at home that's work, but turns into fun
as it becomes like play and there's no way for you to get hurt.

You might lose track of time too but that's a good thing
especially if you start to sing,
since you won't be uptight even if it's in the
middle of the day or late into the night.

The Cure

I've got to do something I know that I must, I've
got to do something to win back his trust.
Some kind of surprise he would never think of.
How about some magic wrapped with a hug?
It may sound strange or extreme
but when you want someone you love you'll do most anything.

This is my goal and my purpose
to get through to my son and not make him nervous.

I've got to do something I know that I must,
I've got to do something to win back his trust.

How it was lost
I don't really know
but what a cost when it happens so slow.
I'll keep trying that's for sure
until I find the special cure.

When that day comes my dream will come true,
when my son says dad I love you.

Oh yeah I've got to do something I know that I must
I've got to do something to win back his trust.

No Regrets

I don't want to die with any regrets
or old lost bets.
I must make a concerted effort every day not to let
any distractions, as small as they may seem
lead me astray from my main dream.
Although I'm sorry this seemingly simple revelation
hadn't occurred in the distant past
I must believe I will last long enough to see all what I want come to pass.
I will now do whatever it takes
to avoid frustrating mistakes
that I used to succumb to
and that I have fortunately learned from so I can quickly continue.
This will help me achieve what I believe should transpire
and give me the peace I truly desire.
I've decided on this new strategy to terminate
what I really hate,
which is losing precious time
on simple obstacles that in retrospect really blow my mind.
For me, and maybe for you too, I must religiously
write down exactly what I want done
and try to make it fun
even if some that is written may seem boring
but must be completed to receive the dream
I'm smitten with and still adoring.

Looking Back

I ate some bread and drank some water, I
stood the old fan up in the corner
and thought I would work until I felt warmer.
Then came a feeling deep within my soul
that caused me to lose half my control.
Memories of long ago seemed to come alive so vividly, in direct contrast
with the death of the past.
Though some were sad and came with regret,
the fond ones helped me to be thankful I could forgive and forget.

What happened to me today was not accidental,
since my fate seemed so rhythmic and influential.
Just by going back to my old workplace I used to call my second home
gave me another perspective as I saw I wasn't really alone.
Although I felt reconnected,
my heart still detected I was partially apart since I sensed what I aspired
seemed so different to what some of them desired.
But that's just fine because in time
I know where my happiness will lie, just as beauty
rests in your eye, I know what's in mine.

The Project

Whenever I take on a seemingly overwhelming project,
I break it into parts so its object is harder to reject. As I catch my breath
and decide what I want to accomplish before my death
I then can pursue the simpler goals that renew my vigor
so old problems won't become any bigger.

While I achieve each small success
with drive and common sense
I will see more happiness being gained with much less expense.
If this is done on a regular basis
then I no longer will be disillusioned with some kind of an oasis,
since my dream will become a reality that can't be
taken away, even any of its smallest traces.

The Steps

I must take all the steps I need that will let all my positive energy flow
and try not to forget what also caused me to sometimes get so low.
As I recapture the spark
that rekindles a youthful heart
I will look forward to any test
that will either bring out my best
or set me on course for what should be next.
Whenever I am in the middle of achieving some goal
I'll remember not to have any expectations which can
quite possibly take the wind from my soul.

Changed Group

The ice had finally been broken
and now the quiet group no longer made softly spoken
whispers of words
they once were so afraid of ever having to be made clearly heard.
There was definitely a noticeable change in their boldness
which decreased their souls coldness,
and a small taste of success was felt as a direct result
from some well welcomed warmness.
It was evident even if they had to play their songs in less than an hour
everything was still fine since they knew they had a renewed power
and were right in time
with their rhythm and rhyme.
Whether they made any money with their
endeavors, they didn't really care,
as long as they could share
what they hoped would never depart
since something was happening in their newly leased hearts.
From observing this I would say if you or me could find a tool
to use
to break an unfortunate stronghold
it should never be abandoned but maybe sold
so all of us can see how it can unfold,
as our old life will finally be dead
and a bright new one can continue being led.

Rest

Although you may think everything
has already been written to sing
or that its all been said before,
I still feel I need to add a little more. I must confess rest
is really the best
first step to most likely undo
anyones confusion they might be going through.
And mine can be so multilayered and oh so thick,
a good sleep always helps me to clearly tick
without any illusional trick.

It is so simple and true
of all things I can or can't do
depends if I'm restored
which then causes me to be either listened to or just ignored.
I'm not just talking about a physical refreshment
I'm talking mainly about a mental testament,
so you can avoid being the fool
who has annoyed the dropout or even the one with the most school.
So if you're a winner
or a societal loser and a sinner
and want to go downtown to have some fun,
make sure that first your thirst for rest
has been addressed
or you may not make it home with any success.
Alone or together,
whatever, after the drive or before
you even open your car door,
since your edginess can come through for sure,
after, during or even right at the start of your fun,
and can always burn you just like the sun.

Hopeful Hearts

Although we may all have some regrets in life, I
believe we can all achieve some success
and not have to settle for too much less
than what we envision ourselves to be at least to some acceptable
level.
Though we may have less time to deal with than
some others, that can really be overrated
since that in itself can cause us to be even more motivated
than before
since it must be compensated for sure.
I guess that's why I like to be surrounded by young or old hopeful hearts
so they can help me spark
my enthusiasm to begin
to emit its light again
like a new candle's flame erasing the shadows
of darkness and pain.
So if you're ever feeling down
about the sound
of your life's story so far,
don't worry
just remember the obvious fact that's hard to hide
but sometimes overlooked, you're still alive.
So it's up to you to change your path from old and boring
to being refreshed and rewarding,
then you can really start soaring
like new
and stop feeling so blue.

What I Think I Need

Though I sometimes like a band's sound,
I don't really need any guitars, drums,
tambourines, or thugs to be around.
I also think I don't really need an accompanying singer that screams
to get my spirit out with my voice and dreams.

If my group clicks then all the other instruments
and things will help us to see and know
our needs will be met with a more extravagant show.
Otherwise what's the point to be involved with
others that don't really see eye to eye
and deep inside they would rather be with other girls and guys.

I guess it's just a matter of time
when I find
my niche by going with my gut feelings and staying focused on plans
and all my dealings with future friends and bands which
can sometimes switch.
I've got to follow through
with all I see as important to pursue in order to be fulfilled in all I do.

Section 3
Religious Poems

The Adventure

I guess one could say I ran away when I was twenty six,
though I wasn't living at home and was in a few cliques,
but was still feeling alone and ready to drift.
I needed something new to get my fix solved
without any silly tricks or fools involved.
Then a pal of mine
said he had a friend who was doing just fine
out west where we could rest
for awhile without a doubt,
and I began to smile while I started to sort things out.
I thought what have we got to lose but our blues
so we headed out west for the coast.
We hoped for the best on our quest for the most
of something we would never regret, or want to forget.
Yes I needed something new to get my fix solved
without any silly tricks or fools involved.
As we rolled away the miles and overcame some trials and temptation
we started to grow tired, but our excitement
about closing in on our destination
kept us wired for the ultimate celebration.
We started to get hungry but we didn't have much money
so we stopped at a church and got some free food, and thanked our Lord
since all we could afford
was the fuel to finish the trip that we just couldn't quit.
Yes I needed something new to get my fix solved
without any silly tricks or fools involved.
As we finally arrived I started to reflect on our adventurous trek
and felt it was a miracle I survived without a broken back or neck.
At that moment I became born again
and thanked Jesus my old friend.
He told me that I will find my peace within and only with him,
and everything will fall into place
while I try to make a contribution to the human race.
Now I know for sure I got my fix solved
without any silly tricks or fools involved.

51

A Closer Bond

I must continue to strive for a closer bond with my Lord
so I won't get bored
with life or almost hypnotized
with things that need to be ignored and not idolized.
I want to really come alive
in areas that once wouldn't survive
and don't want any regrets of what I should or
shouldn't have done in this short life.
If I'm still around 10 years from now I would hate to look back
and not be satisfied for all that
could have been if I had just tried to resist more sin.
For so long I thought I was fine being a loner
until I opened my eyes and realized I could be
much happier being a love donor.

A Good Talking To

Thank you Lord for keeping me free
from all disease and delivering me from all my old insecurities.
In the past I never knew what people meant
when they said during Lent
they got more in return for what they gave up
though it was money already spent
or burned for sure. I was told by these folks it was sparked
by a good talking to from their heart
with you Lord.
Now I see what they really mean
as you open up opportunities for me that I've never seen
before my talk with you Lord. And I know that if I constantly strive
to please and thank you Lord then naturally I will stay vibrantly alive
without feeling doomed during storms since you
will be by my side to help me survive.

Oh Lord I hope and pray I can get your message through to
as many of your children that I can for you.
You know I will do whatever it takes,
either go the extra mile or slam on the brakes
to make them smile for your sakes.
I know when your in me I can do all things through you,
since you've never let me down but have proven
you're always around and true.

Ain't No Saint

Now I ain't
claiming to be a saint,
though I would like to be. I know I make my share
of mistakes, and seem I don't care
as I sometimes backslide
causing my Lord to shake his head
since it doesn't coincide with what his word has said.
I just usually
end up causing myself more misery especially when
I appear a bit cavalier by acting so foolishly.
This is when I get on my knees
to apologize to my Lord as I try to show him my degree
of remorse
for getting so off course.
Then I thank him for letting me take another breath of his air
and feel a desire to please him even more
as he shows me how much he really cares and how he can restore.
Now as for you and where you're at
as far as your spiritual approach or attack
all I can say is give God a chance to be involved with everything you do
so you won't get so self absorbed and feel the world revolves around you.
Remember faith without works is dead
so then grace may not have a face in your life instead.
The emptiness with its thirsts will prevail no
matter what one may do or gain,
you will always feel like you failed just the same.
And your void will always keep you annoyed with pain.
So I feel you must sustain
your faith to regain
your peace so you will live more at ease
and not need
temporary fixes of worldly things
as you digress
in search for some kind of happiness.

Another Level

Well it's back to your mundane job but don't
take it lightly for it keeps you alive
and gives you a ride.
Now if the Lord guides you to the next level, and
you no longer want to settle for mediocrity
but something that gives you more pleasure and security,
then my friend take that chance and find your true destiny.

And if your faith is strong
in our Lord then I'm sure you won't be able to ignore his grace
for long when it's staring you right in the face.
Then you'll see what so many people mean
when they say the Lord spoke to me.
If you get to that point, don't get distracted
and begin going backwards
into sin, just stay on track
without looking back
or thinking of failures of the past that all began from within.

Now sometimes as positive and faith driven as
the path you are now taking can be,
God may make you take a radical turn with
even a better end result for all to see.

Anchoring Power

Although I know my Lord sees me following him in many different ways,
demonic spirits sometimes can still slip in when I'm weary and in a daze,
trying to take me away with envy or anger on any given day.
If not for my Lord's anchoring power
I would hate to see where I could be in my darkest hour.
I have to keep relying on the fact that he has
promises and plans for my life.
For these reasons and really so many more that I know are right,
I then can't let Satan discount any blessings
I have already received for sure
or simply distract my vision from what my Lord still has in store.
Sometimes anxiety will creep in
and then my Lord quickly shows me what I
would reap with a hasty decision.
He shows how it would prevent me from being able
to meet some wonderful people that are stable
or not,
with thoughts that might be equal with mine but may have forgot.

Anticipation

I'm usually not this excited
and I can tell since it's never been this hard to hide it.
I just hope I can relax when I look back
without a chance of having a heart attack.
I think I'm going to be all right
and able to overcome my stage fright
at my first open mic night.
I feel rested and confident
and will use this as my testament
to remind myself and others that you can do anything on God's time table
if you're willing and able.

I say just stay focused and be patient
then who knows who you might live adjacent
to and maybe all your dreams will come true.
You just never know as they say,
but if you ignore this simple cliche you may stay
in your rut with your normal pay.
You've just got to give yourself the benefit of the doubt,
for you might help many others that would love to get out
of their dull routine.
Though it may be steady with a comfortable amount of green,
it may not be their calling for something the world has never seen.

Bad Advice

Whenever I hear the advice
of someone of this world I sometimes unfortunately forget how nice
the Lord's word has been
to me. I then just get frustrated and feel I'm about to sin
as worldly words slip
from my lips
resulting in almost everyone thinking I'm just
too blind not to see what to resist.
I'm grateful now to my Lord that those thoughts and words have departed
and I'm no longer seen as cold hearted
as I was before. My Lord can easily
catch me
before I do something totally foolish or
becoming overly worrisome by appearing too prudish.
He guides me back in line
so I don't have to suffer the cost of losing anymore of life's precious time.
It's really just common sense
that it will be a grave expense
to step further away from our Lord,
which would ultimately be so costly that none of us could ever afford.

Can't Be Denied

I'm so glad my Lord is omnipotent
and that's the reason I feel I will always be
receiving his peace and feeling confident.
I know he will make me more competent
to handle any trial that may come my way
while restoring my smile everyday.
I revel at my Lord's presence in my soul to help me defeat any sin
whenever the attempts of demonic spirits try to
confuse and take control from within.
Some people may say I'm too old to possess some
of the types of dreams I have in my heart
but I don't mind since I have the word of my Lord for my spark.
He also shows me what I need to let go
and what goals to hold on to and let grow.

Can't Give In

Though I'm older now and my dreams sometimes
seem there over when my body aches
and I feel I can't wait any longer,
my Lord gives me the courage to do whatever it takes
with my faith that makes me stronger.

We just can't give in to distractions and sin
since we'll later regret losing our passion from the
light of the Lord that once shined within.
So whenever your life looks bleak
and impure thoughts begin to creep
in, just know it's evil spirits that are trying to seek you out
with doubt
from outside and from within.

When you recognize how subtle and seemingly
justifiable Satan's lies and attacks
can be then you'll have even more reasons to stay on track
with our Lord more powerfully.
Now whenever your feeling down, and the world looks like it's
past you buy, and your alone without a sound in your home,
still give all that you and God love another try
until the Lord decides it's time for you to die,
and takes you home into his heavenly sky.

Clear Up

When I sing some songs it can be just for the art of singing
and not necessarily for its message or meaning.
It can be just for the strengthening of my voice
and I make that practicing choice.

I figure the Lord knows when it's a workout
without a doubt
and where my heart and soul are for a fact.
So I can't let others get on my nerves and distract my mission
of pleasing my Lord as he strengthens my intuition
so I won't be ignored.

I guess to some I may be hard to read
like an old friend I used to know, who did succeed
and had so many different feelings to show. Whether real or not
he could get your attention and make you really think right on the spot.

Comeback Time

I may trip, stumble, or fall,
I may be only able to crawl
but my heart will always be strong for you Lord.
You know I will always comeback
to you somehow
since you taught me what's false, and what's fact before, and now,
and forevermore.
Though storms will come I know and some may
seem to others there's no way out,
but you always eventually show me there is, without ever having to doubt.
I know this is from the peace you offer and that fellow believers
and preachers
have always been talking about.
It's really just a simple transfer of casting all
your cares and worries onto the Lord
which shows him your trust and faith for sure.
So whenever things seem unclear and blurry
and you may start to worry
since a storm is brewing in your life
and you don't know if what you're doing will make things turn out right,
then you've got to ask the Lord for insight
and keep your faith strong
as he will always help you along.
This is when you've just got to leave all your
indecision, all you have and lack to him,
and he will always guide you towards the right path
that you will feel from your gut deep within.

Curious Man

I'm just a curious man
trying to find all my God given gifts to fulfill his plan.
I don't want to leave this earth
never knowing what I was really worth
to him.
I just can't let his light in me go dim
and go back wasting away in sin.

I can just imagine how my last crossroad will appear
as I sense the final day approaching is near
and I'm happy to say I have no fear
thanks to my Lord who's so sincere.

Whenever I have to make my last choice
I hope I have touched others enough with my
Lord's spirit and my hearts voice.
Then when all of us turn back into the earth's dust
we can still live on because of our trust,
faith
and God's beautiful grace.

Driving On

I'm so glad my Lord has sustained my ability
to still enjoy my many interests with the same virility
I did as a boy. I pray this will continue on when I retire
and stay along with me until I finally expire.
Some people think I'm going through a mid life
crisis just since some of my goals seem
like they would be more for the likeness of some teen
who is trying to unfold and grow to overcome their shyness.
I just want to follow God's path of righteousness
to avoid the pitfalls of Satan's schemes with
strongholds that are held by his tightness.
Whatever others think
doesn't bother me since what God has done for
me so far has brought me to the brink
of another level that I will attain,
without disguised help from someone who is suffering from jealous pain.

Thought Control

Every time you think of doing a bad deed
cast it out of your mind and plant a good seed.
As you may know
sin always begins to grow
with a thought while it steals your time and throws
you off.
If you feel your life is headed for destruction,
then I pray you change your ways so your potential can finally function.
I hope my prayer is received
to those in despair that have been deceived.
I'm telling you now what I have found to be fact
and maybe my words will make you react.
Once you obey Gods commands with his thought control,
he will save your sorry soul,
then you can spread whats already been told
in your own way so it doesn't sound old.
And it will touch others and make them feel bold
when they see what their hearts can truly hold!

Foreign Place

Whenever I'm on vacation in some foreign place
without a care or a car in my parking space,
that's when I decide to start a new project out of the blue
or finish an old one that would be rewarding to do.
I thank God for giving me so many interests, which anyone can tell
I like so well.
Fortunately because of this which I also call gifts, doesn't allow my mind
to go back in time
and dwell on thoughts very long which may surface
and have no positive purpose.
Though it's seldom for my thinking to wander into a dark place
and off my usual path since my faith and my Lord's grace
saves me like a true friend,
who will always have my back to my end.

Forgiveness

As I awake
I often wonder how my heart takes
all its abuse and hunger. Maybe it's all just due to
my will to constantly renew my spirit
when only my Lord can hear it.
I just can't let anyone tempt me into a trap
that will just bring back another attack
of pain and loss
at such a great cost.
So for me and maybe you too, I must let my head rule my heart
since I will start
to let my Lord rule my mind
this time as I resign from my selfish controlling thoughts
that always keep me at a loss.
As another day goes by
I will reflect and hope not to cry
for something I may have foolishly said without really knowing why,
I'll now bring it to my Lord every day until I die.

Hanging Tough

Although people can disappoint and baffle me
with lies games and jealousy,
I must forgive as Jesus did knowing we can all backslide
sometimes. I just can't fuss and fret only to later regret
wasting my good energy on anyone
that's angry with me or my family.
I don't want to feel I've been shortchanged caused by my own action
or inaction.
This can cause one to give up on a dream,
so I choose to strengthen my faith in the
greatness of my Lord and the unseen.
As I learn more about my Lord I strive
to be more like him
so I can't afford to backslide and let his light go dim
by losing precious time
with things that don't coincide with his preaching.
I must relinquish any sadness
or madness
by letting my Lord deal
with whoever is trying to steal
away a piece of my mind and just really deserves
God's nerves.
I'm glad I still have a strong enough faith
to wait, though I'm eager to see all his plans he
has for my life through his grace.

Hope and Faith in The Lord

You say there is no way you can get out of the mess you're in,
but I remind you of just where you've been,
and the success you've had
when you thought you were too sad
to take one more night of feeling blue.
Back then hope and faith in the Lord got you through
before and he can do it for you again my friend for sure.
Now if you can see that life's just one huge attitude
with cycles you must embrace with gratitude
even through all of its trials.
Then you will find peace of mind, even when smiles
aren't always on time.
Be thankful you are still here for a purpose
though it may be unclear at times, don't let that get you nervous
or make you blind to your goal
that is still waiting and wanting to unfold.
Stay in tune with the idea that people who are near
to you can help no matter what your pain
may be that seems to be taxing your brain
endlessly. Hope and faith in the Lord will get you through again for sure.
Remember inside you haven't really changed it's just some people around
you can surround you with their opinions which are trying to pound
you into the ground. Their beliefs might be based on half truths or less,
and may possibly gain dominion over your chances of happiness.
This can all be because of your old souls
chip on your shoulder had ticked them off in the past.
Now you have to redeem your self esteem so those bad feelings won't last.
Then you can move on without any chain that's just there to drain
your energy which can hold you back from your need to achieve
what you believe
and preach or even dream you can reach.
Hope and faith in the Lord
will get you through again for sure.

Little and Big Mistake

A long time ago what I just did
would have been something I would much rather have hid.
Back then I thought the action I took
was a big mistake, thinking whenever I might look
back at it in time
and find
all it was lacking
would make it too embarrassing and distracting.
But today it holds almost no weight
since now I have a stronger faith
in the Lord
and know he can't be ignored
when he speaks to me. I'm so grateful that the
same mistake today seems so subtle,
little,
and minuscule
though some I'm sure thought I sounded like a fool.
I know the musical tape I sent my mama
was filled with some trash and would cause some drama,
but I sent it just the same
so there would be no question or blame
of why her request may not have been made.
In a way it was nice to hear her say exactly what I knew she would,
so in that respect it was good
to do what I did
so I could reflect on what I didn't keep hid.
And though she may have thought she had taken the wind out of my sails
she really only made me tougher than some long old nails.

Long Time Coming

It's been a long time since I felt this way
during the holidays,
since I'm usually always running in such a rush trying to avoid delays.
The main thing that made me so happy
was that my boys were both with me, their daddy
and we were all honestly having fun
something I had been longing for ever since '01.
The whole week was great as I also felt so close to my Lord
as my actions poured out for what he wanted me to have explored.
I understand now why so many want to reach this zone
since when you do, it's like God is on the phone
speaking directly to you. It's then when all anxiety and shame is lost
as he frees you of all its pain, with just your faith for the cost.

Every situation
during my holiday vacation
seemed my Lord had his customizing hand right into it.
As no pain was felt since he was with me constantly
while keeping me away from the pit of disharmony.

I will never forget the Christmas of '09
when my sons and neighborhood friends made me feel so fine.
From the ski trip to mammoth mountain with
my good friends Joe and Chris
to the two parties I didn't have to miss.
I also felt calm around a woman I just couldn't resist.
I've just got to thank God for all that wonderful bliss.

Lost Without A Target

I heard her say she was feeling lost, listless, and lethargic,
like a misfit without a target.
I said I had been there before
and was no doctor for sure
but I had a cure
that worked for me
and if she could listen patiently
it might help her find her destiny.

I told her it was something that clicked
with my Lord and me. I was spiraling downward and felt tricked.
But then received a spark
from my Lord real quick and a new start
was beginning for me for sure.
He showed me how to endure
through his word.
I remember it was something like this I heard
as I felt he spoke to me. Sometimes when our complex
problems look as though there is no way to solve them,
a few simple common sense tips can save the day
and our sanity
as we avoid the dips that may lead to a calamity.
There is so much wisdom in the bible
there really is no rival,
and preachers along with other christians who have the
Lord in their hearts can help you see the light
and jumpstart a hapless life.

Moving On After Divorce

As I go out alone now I'm less cold
since I'm finally living part of what I've been taught or told.
I'm beginning to feel hopeful of my gradual recovery
as I make even the seemingly most minuscule discovery.
To some it would likely have no effect but to others
like myself, a small gain to feeling more
the same as before
is monumental for sure.

It's as if I was with someone who made me feel relaxed and serene
instead of upset and mean.
It was like some of my two way street love affairs
when I didn't seem to feel a care in the world
when I was with that special girl.

I know someday she will come around again
whether it's my transformed old love
or someone new sent down from above.
An old friend once said as long as my hope and faith is strong
then some good love should naturally come along.
So I know I can't feel sorry for my lonely soul
just because I haven't yet seen true love unfold.

And if my God feels he can better use me as a
single man then that's what I'll be
since I'm eager to fulfill his plan for me.

My Refuge

Here I am today
back at my little hide away
or as some say my refuge
where I can sort things out and not be deluged
with people who are too confused
and need some time away from. I love this place so I just pray
that someday
I can share it with a woman who can bear it and is tired of being used
or even abused.
Some might say
they don't care how long they may have to be alone and stare into space,
though many of us know the hour is getting late
which in itself can frustrate.
This can bring some of us to the point of bitterness and maybe even hate.
I've decided that's a sad road I choose
not to use,
as I know God will still come through with his loving grace,
as long as I'm true to him. I won't be afraid of how long the wait
may take
or whatever it is that's next for me to face.

Decision Time

Whenever you feel weak
and can't believe you can speak
to anyone about your sin,
just remember God will hear you out without
a doubt and help you always win.
He'll give you the strength you need
to succeed
no matter how large or small the temptation may be.
So why not give God a chance to make things right
in your life, then you will always find
peace of mind in any situation at anytime.
Oh please don't take the risk
of letting your last minute of life tick
away
without allowing any of God's gifts to come into play.
And you know it only takes a split second decision
to resign from your self governing position
so all your potential, can come to fruition.

New Perspective

Sometimes in my confusion and turmoil
I find someone that I think I should almost spoil,
but now I hand this indecision to my Lord
before I lose control and go overboard.
I've found this works best when I look at these occurrences
as a test and not disturbances.
Now that I have a new perspective on these reoccurring pains
I find this elective draws the line.
So I won't have the strain on so much of my energy and time.
This not only pertains to relationships but
anything that you may have trouble
coming to grips with.
Then the peace of finding the right answer from the Lord,
will cease the chances of a possible disaster which you couldn't afford.
I hope these thoughts will transfer to you
and have an impact on all you do.

Pompous Hypocrite

"Are you a pompous hypocrite?"
"Would you ever admit it?" With your nose high in the air,
I can tell you don't even care
but I will still pray for you
to make a breakthrough and see what's really true.
I'm not agreeing with what you think
that I've had too much to drink from your flask
and that I'm really like you only with a different mask
and point of view.
That is just a common comeback from someone who
is off track or maybe half cracked
but I do want to help,
and I'm not here to hurt you with an insult.
I don't want to put you down
and leave here with both of us wearing a frown.
I advise you to try what I did
and not leave anything unspoken, or thinking it's being hid
when you confess to God only some of what you despise
or love. I hope then you can see the lies
that have tripped you up
so much so that you will finally say I've had enough
and truly get in one accord with the Lord.
I believe this way you can begin to change how you think
before you run out of time and be at the brink
of losing your mind.

Pray Time

Please Lord help me out of the mess I'm in,
and forgive me for all my foolishness and sin. I'm worrying so
much of the mistakes I've made ever since I felt betrayed.
Lord, tonight please tell me how I can calm my brain
so I can regain
my true nature and move forward feeling things are all right again.
Help me let go
of what I think I lost since I held on too tight so long ago.
What's that you say? Just put it all in your hands.
Okay then I will just pray and forget my demands,
while letting you and the sands of time work things out,
then I'll be relieved of all my doubt.
I guess once I get in the habit of this routine
then I will no longer stress out on a dream or anything it may be about.

Recovery Time

Now that we have split up, I'll just have to regain my peace of mind.
At least I won't have the stress of someone
fussing at me until the end of time
since it
was just a wrong fit.
My only real worry that I must overcome
is the lack of frequency that I may see my sons.
I will just have to do my best with the cards I have been dealt
and forget any bitterness I may have once felt.
We just have to keep our faith and hope strong and along with our prayers
God will show he cares
in his own special ways. And so often he can leave
us in a daze of happiness and peace,
that's so great we just can't ever let our praise and love for him ever cease.

Reflect and Regroup

As I reflect and see how things went wrong,
I still have my self respect and will remain strong,
no matter how long she stays gone
I will continue to love on and on.
As I detect reasons for different outcomes I see it is not
all my fault for the downfall of my marriage,
so I can't be disparaged
by memories of her frustrated outbursts. I'm
grateful I can continue moving forward
and not let my confidence be lowered
by a replaying of an undeserving feudal combat
like that.
I will just let nature take its course
through this unfortunate chapter of divorce,
as my Lord heals my soul
so I can still live a fruitful life as I grow old.
So now I will just have to take things slow
and not have any kind of anxiety attack for I know
how far that can set me back. I'll just have to
use all the tools at my disposal
so I can eventually make the right proposal
to some one I can love that's likeminded
with our Lord and him being the one who timed it.

The Holy Spirit

Whenever you're weary
and feel you're just too tired and a bit leery
of doing what you really should, then that's when God
can step in and renew your strength so your tongue
won't later spew its regrets in great length.
I must admit
that the Holy Spirit has never let me down or quit
on me and if anything it's been quite the opposite that's true.
So I'm now trying to reduce
these instances to fall between a few and zero,
with the latter to naturally be my goal
so I'll be happier as well as my Lord without
having to deal with another lost soul.

The Right Remedy

I'm so glad my Lord has taught me how I really
can avoid being caught up in sin
by simply listening to him
and how easily it can be
to see Satan flee.
No matter what situation or fix I may be tangled up with, my Lord
knows just the right remedy that will lead to my true serenity.
I can honestly say I've sometimes reached a heavenly state of mind.
It usually happens when I'm in the midst of adversity and I'm still able
to reject what Satan brings to the table.
Whether it's one of his tempting old or new lines
I fortunately know that if agreed with, it will indeed
effect me terribly with obvious ugly signs.
If you ever decide
to quit being stubbornly against our Lord and realize
you can no longer hide from your heart and souls lies
and bad habits
then you will know it is time to give God a fair
try and listen to his commandments.

Changed Fate

With my Lord's help I will never get out of this zone he's put me in with
him since I now know that somehow his righteousness will find a way
to deal with whatever I may face.
This is how I will experience more of his bliss and less time and space
to ponder what I think I miss.
I also can truly relate to anyone who has had their fate change
caused by the disgust of unruly ways
that has kept them down and in a daze,
without anyone around to really trust to come through to save.
Some say it's age and a matter of time
but I don't always agree when I see such a wide
range of believers that stand in line
to sing praises to our Lord,
for all the seekers who are trying to find out how to be in one accord
like a choir that so gracefully puts out Satan's fire, in order to stay cured.

Another Rescue

My Lord, my rock, my best friend
always comes through for me as my prayers were answered once again
so beautifully. I was in the midst of a delicate situation
that was high on my list to be handled by a tempered negotiation
filled with fairness and firmness with no trepidation.
Naturally I religiously went before my God praying knowingly
that he will do what's best for myself and everyone around me.
I asked him to help me with a problem I was having with my eldest son
and for it to be solved smoothly,
without any aftershocks of animosity.
I told my Lord I needed my spare car to be returned from my son to me
and even will offer him payment for a rental fee.
I also explained
that my two week deadline was being strained
and was now only a day
away.
My Lord then said Dave this fourth of July
holiday is yours since it's an even year
so have no fear, just take a drive to their home peacefully,
and the rest just leave to me. So I did and low and behold
I saw both of my sons while they told
me they already delivered my spare car to my door.
I was ecstatic and felt like falling to the floor
but just thanked them over and over before
I had to leave for sure but not to be forgetting to
thank my Lord again and again even more.

Choices

It's not as hard as it used to be
for me to see how things really are with a bit more clarity.
I also now know I must constantly be aware of a distracting spells' glare
with too many painful thoughts that I can hardly bear.
There have been occasions
when I have let some people's life long persuasions
gain a little too much of my time with ideas that never have any true basis
and can even lead to unnecessary tears and hatred.
These days I've really got to stay by my Lord's side to remain
strong and avoid any pitfall everyday that can cause me to stall,
like foolish pride that can last far too long.
My past experiences and instincts have taught me how to pray
so I will be prepared whenever my God chooses it to be my final day.

Second Profession

I'm glad I'm pursuing a second profession
since I know it will help me finally follow through with my past intention.
As long as I'm at peace
and can get sufficient sleep
my Lord will help me succeed in my new business endeavor
while fulfilling my needs with his power and
persistence, for now and forever.
It's been quite some time since I've gotten out
of my rut, and though I've fallen here
and there
I've always gotten back up thanks to my Lord's loving care.

Simplify

All I really have to do is follow through on
the plans I once had that enthused
me to the the point where there was no time to
look back at anything that confused
me. In some areas of my life I have dropped the ball,
this is why I continue to hear my God's call
with a guiding sign
to pick it back up so down the line
my good free will has a chance
to still do another victory dance.
I guess from someone else's perspective on what I need to do
might be an easy selection for them to choose,
only problem is they're not in my shoes.
If you're like me you have chains that others can't see
which compete with your energy
making you sleepy which hinders you repeatedly.
Fortunately
I've found the only way to gain any ground and
rekindle hope and a sparkle in your eye
is to achieve many small goals before giving the big one a try.

Sleepless Hangover

Last night I didn't have a drink
but still got up this morning after not sleeping a wink,
feeling hungover now with my mind on the blink.
Oh Lord rescue me give me rest and tranquility.
I'm tired of tossing and turning,
itching and burning
for all the answers to whatever my heart is yearning.
Stop me from being anxious
and sometimes even jealous. I'll give you all my time as well as faith
'cause I need your loving grace.
Oh Lord rescue me give me rest and tranquility
'cause without you I'll never see the truth,
and I'm sorry I have sometimes failed you for being aloof
in the past,
along with all my schemes that turned into broken
dreams since they just couldn't last.
But this time is different Lord
since I know I can't afford
to lose sight of you anymore, as the final day is approaching
I can't ignore your constant coaching
to help me always endure.
Oh Lord rescue me.

Sometimes Down but Never Out

Thank you Lord for always getting me out of trouble
especially when I really stumble.
I know it's because of you I've gained success
so now I must put my faith to even more of a test
by helping others
as if all the world's men are my brothers
and women my sisters
though some of them may think they're misters
and vice versa due to Satan's confusion
with all of his worldly inertia and pollution.
I'm so glad you've cleared any illusion I may of had
of you, since tonight I felt very alone
until you spoke to me with your power through a phone.
You helped me get over a very dark hour showing
me how much I really hadn't known.
I also see why it's so hard for many to believe in you
God since you're really only best shown
in the hearts of the ones who have repented,
no matter how demented they may have once been,
and so lost in sin.
Oh yes it's a long hard road to hoe, that old straight and narrow path
but it's surely worth it in order to be saved and avoid your almighty wrath!

Sometimes I Wonder

Sometimes I wonder will this be this the summer that I find true love
or maybe it's just going to be another with
distractions from below or above.
Whatever way it ends up,
I'll be happy to know it wasn't just good or bad luck
but by my Lord's will that shows me the self
control that deep down I've got,
and by telling me when to be quiet or not.
I know my God will provide the correct timing for
me to sing my heart and soul with faith
when things look dim or even dark as a black hole in space.
So whenever a positive idea pops into my head
I'll be poised and ready to hear what my Lord has to
say about my thoughts or what I have said. Then I can
take action if necessary or letting it be forgotten
like a flying insect pest needing to be put to rest and left to go rotten.

Temptation

Oh please my friend don't go down that
seemingly inviting and widening path.
It will only lead to your destruction and eventually God's wrath.
It's much better to show your strength with class
by letting all those temptations just pass.
I hope I get through to you today
so in the end you won't have to pay
your debt
with your life in eternal regret.
Oh how you seem so nice
and I know deep down you know what is right,
but you must stand up and fight
even if the attacks are every day and night.
So whenever you feel weary and about to fall,
start to pray and God will hear your call.
Just think what it will all be worth
when you leave this earth,
it's the promised land that awaits for all who kept the faith
and believed in God's grace.

Stay In Line

Whenever I get into a situation where frustration begins to
creep in and teases me like it has so many times before,
I might occasionally act like my old self and panic for sure.
And if that happens I quickly stop myself to pray.
This begins to bring back the new creature God
has made so I can relax and behave,
While realizing his will may be working
mysteriously so I can remain being saved.
Now whatever I was starting to get upset about
and almost causing me to uncontrollably shout
as if I've lost my mind
may not be chosen to be remedied by my Lord
closing in, at this particular time.
It's not because he wants me to continue to carry this anger load
as seen in an unfortunate episode,
but may allow since there may be something he has in store for me,
and somehow this is needed for my eyes to be opened to see.
So sometimes an initial prayer request might not be answered
but be transferred
for something the Lord knows is best for another day
so his greater gift can take a shift to later come into play.
I guess that's where an old saying like "If the Lord's willing" is true
because he may not always be willing for exactly what you want him to do
since he has something greater planned especially for you.

Staying Up

I will not let myself get discouraged over whatever I may lack
since I know my Lord is on my side to help defend me from any attack.
Sometimes all I yearn for is a good nights sleep
to keep me from feeling so wasted and weak.
Other times I just think how much I need
my Lord to take the lead,
since thats what always puts my mind
at ease. It's just a matter of time
when all my dreams will be fulfilled since now I feel
barriers falling that once wouldn't yield.

Thank you Lord

Thank you Lord for walking with me every hour
with your supernatural power
and letting me realize my gifts
while preparing me for your heavenly eternal bliss.
I've been in this position before
but I made too many mistakes and stumbled at your door.
Now today I'm back but it's different this time,
because you renewed my mind
and gave me courage to step right up, and begin to fulfill the life design
you have customized on your time line.
I'm going to come back strong with even more to show
since I really learned my lesson so long ago.
Now if you really want to know how great our Lord is and
really want to get into his business of saving souls,
just let God take control
so you can reach anyone no matter how young or old.

The Concert Flow

Everything seemed to flow so well last night
as I felt the strength of the holy spirit working like a guiding light.
It was great to see and feel
the musical warmths appeal
that was being generated by friendly artists
who orchestrated wonderful voices
along with instruments of their choices.
Anyone could tell that the songs they played
were expressing a wave of hope
that may save someone at the end of their rope.
And even if their music doesn't succeed and materialize
there was still a need being fulfilled in my eyes
and probably others as well if they were to be truly honest with
themselves. I must commend these artists on how uniquely
their dedication
and inspiration to newcomers really is while not getting
a tip or wage they should receive so deservingly.

The Only Way

I must be careful not to get too much rest
when I'm not busy with work as a daily test.
I know I've got to stay alert
so I can preserve all that I am worth to my Lord.
It can be tempting to justify abandoning a project when energy is low
and you just want to relax with the status quo
instead of increasing all your chances to grow.
It's at these critical times
when I pray for extra drive
to get me through both day and night while I
thank God I'm forgiven and still alive.
I must stay close to my Lord so I won't later regret that I didn't really try,
and then look back to see I was only slowly rotting away to die.

The Perfect Answer

Whenever I get a little confused
on which project of mine should first be pursued
I ask my Lord to let me know
of where should I go
and what should I do.
Then everything seems to flow smoothly, falling right into place
so I don't have to worry about precious time going to waste.
Although sometimes it's hard to distinguish
if it's my own thinking
that's advising
or my Lord speaking and really guiding.
One thing that's for sure I can always tell by what's felt
with the end result.
Now some may say that's too late and to some extent
that's true, but with continued prayers being made and sent
you will see patterns in time to help you avoid
your dissent that can make you so blue and annoyed.
You then can increase
your chances of success if you never cease
your quest for becoming more blessed, when your desire
can help you evolve into the woman or man that you aspire.

Ultimate Feeling

I thankfully now see I could have replaced so many tears with laughs,
but back then I took everything so seriously, now at last
I've finally found security.
There really is nothing on earth
that can truly quench all your thirst
and satisfy
like what I have in mind. I'm so happy now I could just cry,
but I will just have to try
and hold all that joy inside this time,
since I don't want to make a scene
and would just like to fulfill a dream.
Have you figured it out,
what I'm talking about
and if not I will stop to tell you here
as to be sure I'm totally clear.
It's that supernatural feeling you can get right now
from God our creator who is somewhere high above the clouds.
And if you have any doubts
just give God a chance to pounce
on any problems you may have in all your remaining days
but remember you must first believe in him
and strive to follow all his ways.

Your Calling

Don't fall into your rival's hands
who try to derail all your plans
and letting him win
by getting under your skin.
It maybe by the stealing of your friends or your ideas,
then you might begin falling back into revenge and sin and all those fears.
Although I may slip and slide into places that should be gone from my life,
I will struggle on when I don't look like a good steward at times.
I will at least know I have my Lord by my side
to get me through whatever storms may break my stride.
When I really believe everything is just a test and a part of his plan
then I will receive the rest and peace I need to become a better man.
Though we all know the fact that life is short,
we can't rush or distort
what we feel is our calling.
It will then only take longer or not occur at all while falling
into our own mistakes
by not letting our Lord's supernatural course take its rightful place.

I Need To Tell You Something

I need to tell you something, and I feel deep down you know it's true.
Where should I start? How can I get through?
Maybe it's with this ... if you've been drifting maybe feeling lost
like somethings missing and can't afford the cost
of another bad decision then you've just got to
listen to what the Lord has to say.
Just give him enough space today
so you can begin believing,
then things will fall into place every season. Yes I need to tell
you something and I feel deep down you know its true.
At first you may not understand the Lord's plan for you
with the setbacks you may have to go through
and bad breaks
you will have to take
to be shaped and ready
for your ultimate destiny.
Simply said, hang in there
even when your life seems it's in the middle of nowhere. Oh yes I
need to tell you something and I feel deep down you know it's true,
so I hope somehow our Lord will finally get through to you.

Mr. Pride

It seems whenever you get close to God you
tend to get complacent and slip,
feeling you can depend on something or someone
else as a replacement to get your fix.
This is what I am finally learning
since I've been born again so many times I probably should be burning.
Today I've decided that this time around
I'm going to use all the tools I've found
over the years
so I won't have to worry about wasting any tears
over doing something I know I shouldn't have
done. Even as strong as I feel today
I know Satan can slip in any one of his infinite different ways.
This is why I can't get over confident with pride and neglect
as this would be tragic without God there to save my neck.

I must give thanks to our God for the past,
present and future since all things
work together for the goodness of one, to those that believe.
That is why I'll never forget his only begotten son
and the supernatural power he can give to everyone.

New Stance

I've decided there is no reason for me to go out on a limb
or bending over backwards for someone I think can't swim,
when in fact they are laughing behind my back in sin.
I'm not saying I'm going to harden my heart, no not at all.
I'm just not going to drop the ball
when I hear my Lord call for me to take his stance
whenever I see the chance
and not to stall
for fools that have already been over ruled and
acting like their back is against the wall.

I believe all of my wishful thinking, and reasoning
for continuing with failed strategies
must disappear to avoid tragedies
without fear of the unknown
by pleasing my Lord so I won't be feeling annoyed, ignored, and alone.
Although I've been taken advantage of in the past
I wont't let a grudge spoil my gifts including the enjoyment of my cash.

Turning the Tables

I must turn the tables and be stronger with my spirit than my flesh
to see what I am truly able to do, after a little peace and rest.
I've had this feeling before and have sadly slipped or backslid as some say
but I will never stop trying to fulfill the plans my Lord has for me today.

Though I've stumbled
and then later grumbled
about how could I have fallen off track,
I still get a thrill of my Lord calling for me to come on right back.
When I compare myself with the way I was
in both the near and distant past
I can see changes that I pray will continue and hope will always last.

Never Get Rattled

You can lead
yourself to believe you need
or want something or someone when you really don't, since your mind
can easily be thrown off when you find
you're consumed with this,
then confused with them
or it again and again.
Sometimes these thoughts can be true but they often are not
since most people have forgot
to put God first in their lives.
So whatever thrives in their eyes
will eventually leave them feeling empty
when they've reached what a false master has preached to many.
Although I love these misled souls as much
as my christian brothers or sisters,
they may never let me get as close to them as I wish, since my belief differs
I know,
just like a clashing side dish that doesn't really go.
Unfortunately more often than not this may be the case today
but this won't cause me to to lose the smile on my face or fade away.
I don't believe becoming overbearing or self
righteous is the way to approach
a non believer, but just sharing as a standby friend or coach
when they come in need seeking advice and
hope is probably the best play to call
for most of them all.

Section 4
Characters

Courtney

I met a sweet woman just yesterday,
but sadly for me I think she is gay.
I guess I will still have to wait and have patience
'till I find my dream date or just another acquaintance.
But now that doesn't mean I wouldn't like to be her friend
even if it may seem frustrating every now and then.
For some strange reason
I keep believin'
our spirits can overcome
anything under the sun.
I sense we have some common ground
so I would like to pursue what I feel I might have found.
She loves music as I do
and writes and plays so tenderly and true.
I hope she calls some day
to listen to what my songs have to say.
Maybe together we will find just in time the right sound to play
to uplift others when they're feeling down and about to stray.
There's an unfortunate chance she was just being polite
the other night and has no interest in my songs no matter what I write.
If so then once again I'll tell myself I'll be fine
and just move on down the line
to meet another woman musician
who would like to better her position and mine
by getting together more than one time.

Retirement Eve

Retirement Eve has come and passed away,
now it's our old friend Joe's final day.
Will he reminisce soon hereafter
or will it be sometime when he's long out to pasture!
A colorful man was he,
with his pretentious style and comedy
that sometimes seemed to border on insanity!
When you first come across Joe he may be hard to read,
with him always wearing his emotions on his sleeve,
but none the less he will surely be missed,
even if there were moments he made you want to shake your fist!
Sometimes you may have thought to yourself, is he really sad
or mad
or just joking endlessly,
but whatever the real answer may ultimately be,
it doesn't really matter because now he is free!

Section 5
Political Poems

It's Open Mic Geek Night

So many geeks wear suits and ties
especially politicians with all of their lies.
Some come across under the guise of a christian
but really they're just fakes with half their brains missin'.

Now God says love your enemy and people you may despise
since it doesn't take much effort to love someone
thats been loving you all your life.
So here I stand to feel what a politician does
wearing a suit and behind a mic
trying to make an impression on everyone whether
they lean to the left or the right.
But as I look down at my speech
I'm starting to think who will I really reach.
I know my jaws will start getting tired
and I may not get the applause I desired
by sensing my speech might being going south
since it sounds like I will be talking from both sides of my mouth.

Liberal Christians

Some people say the closer you get to God the closer you get to your grave.
As liberal christians today we say
though this may be true in some cases,
we can't be afraid of death, and it won't be shown
within our soul or on our faces.
This my friend is since its sting has been taken away
from a believer who nears their end whenever, or even today.
As long as we have traces of faith everything will
be fine in the unseen and unknown
which will allow us to bend but not break with the seeds we have sewn.
We all have the freedom of choice, and since we all must
carry our own cross and not others, then we shouldn't
force our belief on our sisters and brothers.
We will then just become a nuisance
like some kind of pollutants,
that will just drive them away, making them seem aloof from us,
even if we're speaking the truth enough.
As we believe in the separation of church and state,
we still leave our doors open to anyone who fears
their choices may destroy their life and fate
if they continue with their evil ways without the light today.
If anyone should choose to come join us at God's table
we will be willing and able
to accept them with love and show them that they are forgiven
for whatever they may have done, while helping them in their
transition in believing the Lord and his only begotten son.

About the Author

I've always been more of an introvert than an extrovert, however I can adapt like a chameleon when necessary. Since my nature is to internalize and analyze, I found great satisfaction in writing and especially writing poems that rhyme. For me it all started back in 2001 when I started keeping a journal as a way to vent. It then began to escalate into poetry as I began to heal. I liked how much writing was helping me to become happier and decided to make it more challenging by  making my writings rhyme. It to me was and still is like a puzzle for me to complete. I hope my enjoyment from writing these poems will translate into your enjoyment from reading them.

Printed in the United States
By Bookmasters